D0349957

To:

From:

THE
CATKINS
DIET

Get more meat from humans!

Feel better about being a "house pet"

Uncross your lives from 9 to 16 or more!

Be able to nap at will!

Felix Catkins, DVM

Dr. CATKINS
DIET
REVOLUTION
Felix Catkins, DVM

Felix Catkins, DVM

Translated into human by Michael W. Domis

Peter Pauper Press, Inc.
White Plains, New York

To our little dude—Gus

Illustrations copyright © 2005 Studio 2

Designed by Taryn R. Sefecka

Copyright © 2005
Peter Pauper Press, Inc.
202 Mamaroneck Avenue
White Plains, NY 10601
All rights reserved
ISBN 1-59359-980-3
Printed in China
7 6 5 4 3 2

Visit us at www.peterpauper.com

THE
CATKINS
DIET

Get more meat from humans!

Feel better about being a "house pet!"

Increase your lives from ? to 18 or more!

Be able to nap at will!

Felix Catkins, DVM

Dr. CATKINS
DIET
REVOLUTION
Felix Catkins, DVM

CONTENTS

WARNING!!!

The following manual is intended for cats' eyes only. If it should fall into the hands of humans, we cats would lose our tactical advantage in their world, and the secret revolution to make humans our slaves through the discreet use of cute aloofness would be set back by at least 100 years. So, safeguard this with all nine of your lives.

THE PROMISE

Catkins is more than a diet—it's a revolution. A revolution that involves, as do all revolutions, upsetting the balance of power in your world.

Get more meat from your humans and more protein in your diet! Feel better about being a "house pet"! Increase your lives from 9 to 18 or more! Be able to nap at will! (On second thought, we do that already. Never mind.)

This book can show you how to do all this and more by simply training your humans to bend to your will.

If you're like most cats, you've probably been through the protein-loss wars. You've been subjected to all manner of disgusting dry food from your humans simply because they think you'll like it because it comes in "little fishy shapes." Like we cats care what our food looks like. Really, now. Or, you've been subjected to canned, reconstituted, carbohydrate-laden food

with cutesy names like "Feline Feast" or "Gourmet Grill." Don't let the names fool you. It's still . . . garbage.

Oh, I'm sure you've gotten the occasional meat treat from your humans. They probably buy a random can of wet cat food when it's on sale, or when they think about it, but, if you're like most cats, you've been reduced to either eating the dry stuff, or begging scraps from the table. I know the really destitute among us have taken to, ugh, hunting again.

But, I ask you, did we really invade the humans' lives just so we could do what our cave-cat ancestors were forced to do to survive? No, of course not. We invaded to make OUR lives easier, not theirs. After all, they weren't the ones who were worshiped in Egypt, now were they?

Let's face facts, here. Humans are, by and large, lazy tubs of goo. And, their laziness is really hurting your eating habits. So, you have to change THEIR mindset. Remember, you are the cat, and you are in charge.

THE TWO
PICTURES

Since a picture is worth a thousand words, here are two that you can think about before committing to the Catkins Diet Revolution.

I see you, the cat, sitting in front of a giant bowl of meat, or fish, or chicken in gravy, or eggs Benedict. Beside the bowl of meat, I see another huge bowl of warm, sweet cream. Isn't that a nice picture?

But wait, there's more. If you act now, and get with the Revolution, I see a picture of you, fur shining, eyes glowing, with your "owner" standing beside you. Your "owner" is saying something. Can you hear it?

"Whatever Kitty wants, Kitty gets. Would Kitty like more meat? Or cream?"

Oh, my, aren't those the most wonderful pictures?

CHANGING YOUR
CATTITUDE

'm sure by now that several questions have popped into your furry little head. Let's address them.

1. Is this diet safe?

For you? Of course. For your human? Right. Like you care. If old Tubbo double-dates with the Grim Reaper while bending over with the bowl of meat, just go get another so-called "owner."

Helloooooo! Earth to Cat. It's MEAT! It's what we live for.

Are humans perfect? Of course not. The Catkins Diet Revolution requires a lifetime commitment to changing your human's habits for your benefit. But remember, you can do this; you're the cat.

14

THE FOUR PRINCIPLES OF THE CATKINS DIET REVOLUTION

1. *You will get more meat from your humans.* The cats who follow the regimen in this book invariably increase their meat intake by as much as 1,000%. For those cats cursed with living with truly dim owners, a future chapter will outline some anarchist tactics designed to swat even the stupidest human into line.

2. *You will maintain a high level of meat in your diet.* We know that there are cats who have tried other methods of training humans, and have had initial success, only to have their humans backslide. Well, this is where the Catkins Diet Revolution leaves all the other programs in the dust. We'll show you, step by step, how to irrevocably alter your human's behavior so that it most benefits you.

3. *You will achieve better health.* Face it, cats aren't meant to eat veggies and carbs. We're meant to eat meat. Meat good; carbs bad. Once you slough off those Kitty Krunchies, your energy, vitality, and sex appeal will skyrocket. Your friends (or littermates) won't believe how good your fur looks.

4. *You will lay the groundwork for disease prevention.* Not only disease prevention, but death prevention. If you do this right, you'll never have to go outside and hunt again. Outside is where the diseases are. Outside is also where the vehicles are. We all know, from reading the Cat-bituaries, how many of our unfortunate brethren and sistren have gone to that Big Cat House in the Sky from chasing meat into traffic.

FOOD CATEGORIES

Humans may just be getting around to high protein, low carb diets (they are a little "slow," after all), but cats have been eating like this for years (or at least until the invention of kibbles). For the purposes of the Catkins Diet Revolution, what cats eat can be divided into categories.

We're talking meat, poultry, fish, eggs, and dairy. It's what we eat. It's the best food for cats. If you have found yourself irritable or lethargic, chances are you have been missing the complete dietary protein found in these foods. Whether freshly dead, or slightly moldy, it should be the main (99.9% at least) staple of your diet.

All meats are good, but some are better than others. Fish is the best choice for any cat, but be careful. Read the label on the tuna can to make sure it's dolphin safe. It's not that we care about dolphins, it's just that you shouldn't mix your fishes. Dolphin has a delightful, piquant flavor and should be eaten all on its own.

One caveat about meat, though: avoid roadkill. Only low-class felines eat from the "asphalt buffet."

Every cat needs a little something to wash the meat down. Don't drink too much, however. Cream is fattening, and a fat cat is an unintentionally lazy cat. Keep yourself lean to keep your humans in line.

3. Crud

Anything that your humans serve you that's not protein or cream falls into this category. It's loaded with energy-sucking carbohydrates and all manner of unhealthy chemicals. Crud is to be assiduously avoided.

BARRIERS TO
SUCCESS

1. Physical Barriers

OK, in order for this to work, you have to put some effort into it. I know we used to be worshiped in ancient Egypt as gods, but that was a long time ago. You now have to get up off your furry butt and use your natural cunning and overwhelming intellectual superiority to re-train your humans. Got it? Nap time is over, for now.

2. Psychological Barriers

You should have none. You're a cat. Humans are the ones who visit psychologists and psychiatrists, not us. If you do have "owner issues," call the Cat Crisis Hot Line at 1-900-myhumanisadork, and ask for Tabby. (It will be discreetly billed to your owner's phone at only $5.99 a minute.)

If you *do* have issues, tailor them to your advantage, as follows:

BODY IMAGE. Change the way you look at your body—think Garfield!

FOOD OBSESSIONS. Are you the type of cat who nurses on the teddy bear when no one's looking? You may have an oral fixation—work it, baby!

THE BASICS OF
CATKINS

In this chapter we will show you some basic maneuvers to let your humans know that you are unhappy with their choice of food.

Before we begin, however, I must tell you that these maneuvers work only on ordinary humans. There is a class of human that will never, ever, feed a cat meat:

vegetarians. If you happen to find yourself living with such a human, do the smart thing: move out. Find a nice meat-eating family. We cats didn't claw our way to the top of the food chain to eat tofu, OK? 'Nuff said.

SCENARIO #1:
Your human places dry
food in your bowl.

Maneuver:

Run to the bowl. Twist and twine excitedly around his legs while loudly vocalizing. Sniff the food. Look at your human. Sniff the food again. Look at your human again. Sit, with your back to the food. Look at your human again. Do NOT, under any circumstances, eat what is in the bowl. When your human starts saying inane things like they always do ("Look. Fresh kitty num-nums. Isn't Kitty hungry?"), look longingly at the bowl, move in to take a bite, and . . . walk away.

After the human leaves, wait five minutes. Then, sit in front of the bowl and cry. When your human comes to investigate,

look longingly at the bowl and complain, loudly. Walk away. Wait for the human to leave.

Repeat.

Eventually, even the dimmest humans will figure out that you don't like the food. Ideally, this will force them into a cycle of buying new food to find one that you like. Of course, if it's only dry food that they buy, you mustn't like any of it. The goal here is to get them to buy wet food, first. It's not meat, but it's a step in the right direction.

A word of caution about canned cat food: it's only good if it lists meat as the first ingredient. To ensure that you're getting mainly meat, wait until your owner goes to sleep, and then read all the cans in the cupboard. Meat should be listed as the first ingredient. If it's not, throw the can out, or hide it under the couch.

And, never, never, never let on that you can read. If humans find out that we can read, the revolution will fail.

Now, I realize that your human can go through several different brands of dry cat nuggets before stumbling on the realization to buy canned. This presents a problem for you: How do you survive on only dried food, and yet leave your humans with the impression that you're not eating?

The answer is surprisingly simple. Wait until the human is asleep, or out of the house. Eat one nugget per hour, only. In this way, the bowl will look full for at least a week. This is usually long enough for even the most hard-headed human to realize that you're not eating the food, and he should try something else.

If, however, your human doesn't comply after a week, more drastic measures must be taken. It is at this point that we would suggest introducing fiber into your diet—specifically, grass.

Consume some dry cat food, then go out and consume some grass. Come back in, sit on your human's lap, and give him back the dry cat food, and the grass, if you know what I mean.

It only takes a time or two of doing this for him to figure out that he should try a different cat food. Be careful, though. If you do this too often, it could get you a quick trip to the vet from a nervous owner. No cat wants that.

SCENARIO #2:
Your human is eating meat.

Maneuver:

Place yourself on the floor, and be sure you are in his line of sight. Stare at him, lovingly. Remember, make big eyes, preferably big moist eyes. Meow soulfully. This should be enough to dislodge a scrap or two from your human.

If not, more aggressive action must be seriously considered.

Sit patiently by your human. Don't move; don't talk. As the human brings a forkful of meat to his mouth, stretch up and put your paws on his leg. Now, meow with your most pitiful voice. That voice, combined with your gentle, loving touch, should get you some meat.

However, there are those truly stubborn humans who refuse to bend.

For one of them, sit patiently and quietly by his legs. As the forkful of meat moves toward his mouth, stretch up and put your paw on his leg, as before. Now, just before the meat reaches his mouth, extend all ten claws and DIG, BABY, DIG!!! This is always startling enough to cause him to drop the fork. Grab it and run. Granted, you only get one piece of meat out of this, and one annoyed human, but, hey, he has a short memory. He'll forgive you in no time.

ADVANCED CATKINS

What follows are a few techniques to ensure that you get even more meat than your humans are willing to give you.

1. The Grocery Bag Shuffle

Watch for when your human returns from

the store. Wait out of sight just inside the doorway. When he enters the house, dart between his legs, pausing long enough to trip him. The bags he is carrying should crash to the floor, spilling their contents. While the human is dazed and confused, quickly grab whatever meat is in the bag and stash it under the couch for later. After, lie innocently on the floor and groom. Wait until the mess is cleared and the human goes out for the next batch and repeat.

Most humans will prepare some kind of meat for supper. Wait until the meat is out on the counter, and the human turns around to get something. Using your Cat-astrophic Speed™, snatch the meat off the counter, eat it, and return to your previous position on the floor. Remember, humans think we are super fast only if there's danger around, so don't let on that you can move like this whenever you want. And, for your sake, don't giggle when the human looks confused about where the meat went.

Leave dead prey beside the bag of kibbles. It makes a strong statement.

Wait until the humans are sleeping, then use your razor-sharp claws to excise a small section of the refrigerator door gasket. Without a vacuum seal, the fridge door will swing open to reveal a sumptuous buffet.

CATKINS FOR MULTI-CAT HOUSEHOLDS

Fortunate indeed are those cats who share their home with another. This is the surest sign that the cats are in charge. Getting meat to eat in a multi-cat household should be easy. Just follow the advice above. While some humans can resist the charms and wiles of one cat, two cats or more are just too adorable for them to resist. You'll be eating meat and cream out of their hands in a week with very little effort.

To supplement, however, you could try using the Bait and Switch technique. It works particularly well when the human is making dinner. One cat must distract the human. Use cuteness if need be, but simple meowing will often do. Once the human turns in your direction, your partner, using Cat-astrophic Speed™, slips in behind, snatches the meat, and stuffs it under the couch. Later, you and partner can enjoy the meat at your leisure. For an added treat in the wintertime, wait for the human to leave and then cook the meat over the furnace grate. It takes a while, but it's yummy.

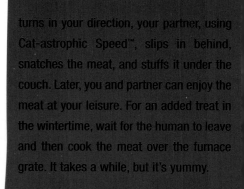

CATKINS
AND DOGS

Even the best of us occasionally is saddled with a human who likes dogs. Don't worry about it, OK? If you can bend a human's will to your own, bending the dog's will to your own should be as easy as sandblasting a cracker.

A quick hiss and spit should be enough to get "Fido" to move over and give you a peek at his food bowl. Eat the meat and leave the rest.

You can also leave any food you don't like for the dog. They'll eat anything. Don't believe me? When was the last time you saw a cat dining at the Litter Box Buffet?

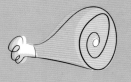

CATKINS
DAILY REGIMEN

Catkins isn't just a revolutionary diet, it's a lifestyle. You've inducted your humans into the program and worked to shape and maintain their new feeding habits. Now, for lifetime maintenance . . .

The following chart will help you decide what to eat, and what to avoid.

EAT REGULARLY

stuffed trout	cream
bacon	cold cuts
veal chops	pâté
crab cakes	cheese cubes
filet mignon	ice cream
chicken kabobs	lobster
cheese omelets	sausage patties

EAT SPARINGLY

kibbles	starches
vegetables	soy products
fruit	fiber

53

Meal tips:

You can use the following sample menu as a daily dietary guide and live in perfect health and harmony:

BREAKFAST:
Bacon & eggs

MORNING SNACK:
duck pâté, cream

LUNCH:
chicken consommé,
shrimp scampi

MIDDAY SNACK:
foie gras, warm milk

DINNER:
sardine appetizer,
grilled lamb chops

EVENING SNACK:
herring in cream sauce

cream

RECIPES

For your meat-eating pleasure, we have enlisted the services of Chef Butch O'Malley, owner and operator of Le Chat Chat on the Green, to whip up some delicious recipes guaranteed to please even the most finicky palate.

Today's Menu

Breakfast
meat

Morning snack
cream
(meat optional)

Lunch
meat
(cream optional)

Midday Snack
cream

Dinner
meat

Pollo con Crema

Cook chicken
(or don't—your choice).

Put in bowl.

Cover with cream.

Eat.

Boeuf avec Crème

Cook beef
(or don't—your choice).

Put in bowl.

Cover with cream.

Eat.

Creamy Lamb

Cook lamb
(or don't—your choice).

Put in bowl.

Cover with cream.

Eat.

Pig in a Blanket

Cook ham
(or don't—your choice).

Put in bowl.

Cover with a thick
blanket of cream.

Eat.

Beef Stew

Fill bowl with cream.

Add as many beef
cubes as you'd like
(cooked or uncooked).

Stir.

Eat.

CATKINS AND EXERCISE

Exercise is important—for others, of course. Cats are perfect. If, however, you feel the need to supplement your daily regimen of playtime and being worshiped with a little physical activity, keep in mind that you should wait at least two hours after eating before strenuous exercise. Therefore, if you eat the recommended three meals and three snacks a day, that leaves only between 11:00 P.M. and 7:00 A.M. for your exercise routine. And, whatever you do, make sure the humans know that you're exercising. Make it loud, and make it proud, cats and kittens.

As usual, before beginning any exercise program, you should make sure the humans are out of the room. (That's why you have to be LOUD!!!)

For exercise, we recommend the following:

Stretching exercises

The first exercise you should attempt is stretching. It's always good to keep those muscles limber for snatching and grabbing meat.

To begin, stand with all four paws on the carpet. Reach out with your front paws, extending your claws to hold onto the carpet. Now, streeeetch. Really reach for it, now. Get in a little digging action, too. Can't afford to let those claws get dull. Excellent. Relax.

Take a deep breath and stretch one leg out behind you. Way back, now. Stretch it. Come on. You can do it. Now, hold it. And . . . release. Good. Now the other leg. Really reach for it, now. Don't be lazy. Hold it. And . . . release. Way to go.

One more stretch. Arch your back. Hunch up and stick that back up in the air. Really high now, come on. You can do it. Higher. Higher. Great.

Now, relax, settle back down on the carpet, and . . . nap. After stretching like that, a good 30-minute nap just hits the spot, doesn't it? Enjoy.

Muscle Building Exercises

While we all know that cats don't need to exercise to be in good shape, it's not a bad idea to bulk up those muscles. With good muscles you can shave nano-seconds off your Cat-astrophic Speed™ times and you might even qualify for the Cat-lympics.

So, here are a few time-tested exercises for getting those flexors and extensors in shape.

THE CLAW

Find the newest piece of furniture in the house. Stretch up as high as you can and dig all 10 claws into it. Very slowly, so as to get the maximum burn out of the muscles, pull down, dragging your claws through the furniture. Repeat at least twice.

Next, stretch as high as you can, dig those claws in again, and use short, pulling motions. Repeat at least twice.

As your muscles get stronger, you can increase the number of repetitions.

In no time at all, you will have whittled that furniture down to toothpicks and your claws and forepaw muscles will be the envy of the neighborhood. Nobody will ever kick kitty litter in your face again.

PULL-UPS

This is an excellent exercise to improve not only your forepaw strength, but your abdominal muscles as well.

Stand in front of the new drapes in the house. Jump as high as you can, and dig your claws in. Hang. Relax.

Now, release your back claws and slowly pull yourself up to the top bar of the curtains. Walk along the top bar until you can jump onto the credenza and back onto the floor.

Repeat as least five times to start.

THIGH BURNERS

Here's an easy way to give yourself those lovely, leonine thighs that every cat desires.

Wait until the humans are asleep. Go to any corner of the house. Hunker down.

On your mark. Get set. RIP!!!

Race, at top speed, from one end of the house to the other. Do NOT worry about banging into things or knocking things over. Fallen detritus makes an excellent obstacle course for the next lap.

Pause at the other end of the house. Make sure the humans have gone back to sleep. Repeat.

We recommend this exercise be done not more than three times to start. If you repeat it too often, the humans are likely to get too annoyed and throw you outside.

Now, while this is excellent exercise for any cat, cats who are fortunate enough to live in two-story structures can really build up those leg muscles by incorporating the stairs into their nightly rips.

A word of caution, however. Never rip down the stairs. Even the most graceful cat has been known to go ass over teakettle when racing down a flight of stairs. While most things in the universe favor cats, gravity doesn't. Which is why gravity sucks.

CONGRATULATIONS!

Remember those two pictures I drew for you at the beginning of this book—the ones in which meat and cream became your just desserts, and entrees, too. Well, if you've followed my advice, you are ever so much closer to making them a reality.

Look at yourself in the mirror. You're one good-looking feline, aren't you? Well, you always were, but, using the Catkins

Diet Revolution, you are now the Top Cat of the House, no matter what house you're in.

It's a good feeling. Strut your stuff, kitty-cat. Be proud. But, don't let your guard down. Remember, they still think they "own" you. Foolish humans!

Get more meat from humans!

Feel better about being a "house pet!"

Increase your lives from to 18 or more!

Be able to nap at will!

Felix Catkins, DVM

Dr. CATKINS
DIET
REVOLUTION
Felix Catkins, DVM

LONG LIVE THE
REVOLUTION!!!

Felix Catkins, DVM